WARTIME VIGNETTES

WARTIME VIGNETTES

A Boyhood Memoir of World War II and of Its Aftermath

T. A. DOLOTTA

Copyright 2017 by T. A. Dolotta
All Rights Reserved.

All rights exclusively reserved. No part of this book may be reproduced or translated into any language or utilized in any form or by any means, electronic or mechanical, including photocopying, recording or by any information storage and retrieval system, without permission in writing from the publisher.

Published in the USA by:
Uniflow Press

Dolotta, T. A.
Wartime Vignettes
A Boyhood Memoir of World War II
and of Its Aftermath

ISBN 978-0-9991246-0-4 (paperback)
       978-0-9991246-1-1 (hardback)
       978-0-9991246-2-8 (ebook)
Library of Congress Control Number: 2017946607

Book design by T. A. Dolotta
Copy Editor: Lynn Jones Green

Cover/interior design

AquaZebra™
Web, Book & Print Design
www.AquaZebra.com

Persons mentioned in this book have given their permission to the author to use their names.

10 9 8 7 6 5 4 3 2 1

DEDICATION

This book is dedicated to the memory of my aunt, Dorka Elencwajg; of my parents, Dwojra and Nathan Elencwajg; of my wife, Barbara Hamstrom Dolotta; and of the more than twenty other close members of my family who were murdered by the Nazis.

T. A. Dolotta

DISCLAIMERS

I was motivated to write this narrative for my family and my friends, to tell them how the horrors of the Holocaust and World War II were perceived by me as a young boy. I want to assure the reader that I have reported, to the best of my ability, all the events described here as accurately as possible. However, given that those events span primarily a range of some thirteen years—from the year that I was five through the period when I was seventeen—and that I am aware of a few of those events only because I learned about them later, second-hand, it is conceivable that my memory may have betrayed me, and that some inaccuracies may thus have crept into this narrative. If this did indeed occur, I take full responsibility for it, and I ask for the reader's forbearance.

I also want to inform the reader that the primary purpose of the references listed at the end of this book is to provide additional perspective on, and corroboration of, the events described here.

The dates of some of the included photographs are approximate.

Finally, I want to thank the members of the Creative Writing Group at Maravilla in Santa Barbara, California, for their help in editing this narrative.

T. A. Dolotta

TABLE OF CONTENTS

1. Prologue 1
2. On the Run 9
3. The Russian Commissar 15
4. Aunt Dorka 21
5. Uncle Heniek 27
6. A Fork in the Tracks 35
7. In Hiding 41
8. Goodbye, Warsaw 47
9. The Young Soldier 55
10. VE Day 61
11. Back to Warsaw 65
12. New Exodus 71
13. Epilogue 81
14. Photographs 89
15. Map of the Relevant Area 97
16. References 99

-1-
PROLOGUE

I turned five years old just two months before Nazi Germany started World War II by attacking Poland on September 1, 1939. At the time, my parents and I lived in Warsaw, Poland.

Both my parents were raised and educated in Kielce, a mid-sized town south of Warsaw. After high school, my father went to law school at Jagiellonian University in Kraków. My mother went there as well; she told me later that she did so to keep an eye on my father and to make sure that no other woman "stole" him. After law school, my parents got married and settled in Warsaw, where my father started to practice law; his was a solo practice and his office was in our apartment; he had no secretary. My mother started her own business; it was an early version of Kinko's: typing, copying, etc. It also provided translation services from some fifteen languages to and from Polish; she employed over thirty translators. I think her firm was the only one that offered this sort of service in Warsaw, and it was very successful.

Our household consisted of my parents and me; my nanny Irenka ("Irenka" is the Polish diminutive of "Irene") who was also our housekeeper; my father's mother, Hannah; and my father's sister, my Aunt Dorka. My aunt's first name was actually Dwojra (Dorothy), but that was also my mother's name. To avoid confusion, my aunt became Dorka — a diminutive of Dwojra, because she was younger than my mother — and all was well. She was a huge help in taking care of my grandmother and me. Because my mother worked, Dorka was effectively my surrogate mother. She and my grandmother occupied a part of our apartment: a small kitchen with a pantry, and a dining nook, a bathroom, a bedroom, and a sleeping loft for Irenka.

We all shared our huge living/dining room; that room was big enough for me to ride my two-wheeler child's bicycle in. Whenever I rode that child's bicycle in the street, I created a commotion, because such bicycles were unknown in Poland. I had one because my mother bought it for me in France when she went to the 1937 Paris World's Fair.

While I was a baby, Irenka took me to my mother's office twice a day so my mother could breastfeed me. After I turned four, I was in charge of answering the phone whenever no one else was available. I was our "voice-mail" machine; such machines did not yet exist. The arrangement worked pretty well: Irenka would put me on my potty, put the phone on the floor next to me, and I was all set. When the phone rang, I would answer it, saying something like, "Hello, no one is here." During my typical "work shift" of half an hour or so, I'd receive at most one or two calls, which I could easily remember.

My grandmother was in poor health. She had the good fortune to die about a month or so before the start of World War II. She had already survived World War I, and had she lived through World War II, or even a part of it, I believe she would have suffered a great deal.

A few days before the start of World War II, my father, who was a lieutenant in the Polish Army Reserves, received orders to rejoin his unit in eastern Poland. He took his helmet and his uniform, with all the medals he had received in the Polish-Soviet War of 1919–1920, cleaned out his rifle, his sidearm, and his bicycle, and pedaled east. After that, we lost contact with him for about six months, but then we found him (see below). The Polish army was being badly beaten at that time by the Russians and my father, who was then a soldier with the Polish army, was ordered to retreat. He walked from Kiev in the Ukraine to Warsaw, over five hundred miles; he told me that, while walking that distance, he taught himself to sleep while walking.

Now only four of us were still together: me, my mother, Dorka, and Irenka. I was "the man of the house."

Except that Germany started a war with Poland on September 1, 1939, and very soon there was no house. By the next morning, our five-story apartment building at 8 Graniczna Street had been reduced by the Luftwaffe (German Air Force) to a pile of broken and pulverized bricks. No trace was left of our apartment, or my bicycle, or my piano, which my mother wanted very much for me to learn to play. My piano teacher was killed in the German bombing air attacks (he was the first of several of my piano teachers who met this fate during World War II). It was the start of the German Blitzkrieg ("lightning war"). By the end of September, the Germans had occupied the western and central parts of Poland, while the Russians occupied the eastern part, as secretly agreed to earlier by their respective foreign ministers, Ribbentrop and Molotov. In the area occupied by the Germans, there was a shortage of food, no running water, practically no heat (and it was a Polish winter!), and in Warsaw many of the houses were totally destroyed. We stayed for one or two nights at a time with friends, or with people who were willing to rent us a room or, more rarely, two rooms. I kept count of the different places I had slept in since the start of the war. I stopped counting when this count hit about eighty after six or seven months.

Occasionally, there was some horse meat to eat. Once, we stumbled, in an abandoned warehouse, upon a cache of canned food, lots of French wine, and lots of tea. Strange diet.

-2-
ON THE RUN

Around January of 1940, the Germans announced that they would build a ghetto to house the nearly half-million Warsaw Jews (Warschauer Ghetto — the largest Jewish ghetto ever). My mother's reaction was simple: "We will not go into a ghetto on my watch!" She was wrong.

We prepared to smuggle ourselves into the eastern part of Poland, which was occupied by Russians. The border between these two parts of Poland was the Bug River. It flows roughly from south to north, and passes near Tręblinka, the location of a major extermination camp. We were told that the Bug was easily crossed at night, because at that time of the year, it was already frozen solid. So around February of 1940, we set off to the east, led by an appropriately-bribed guide. All the adults in our group wore dark clothes that were hard to see. I wore a white rabbit's-fur coat, so I shone like a beacon and made a perfect target for the German border guards. Bullets started whistling past us. Fortunately, my mother realized what was happening and took off her black coat and threw it over me. The shooting stopped.

Without any other misadventures, we reached the eastern edge of the river and ran for our lives until we found ourselves far enough from the river's edge to feel safe. We kept going east—mostly on foot—until we got to Białystok, a mid-size town in eastern Poland.

By April 19, 1940, the Warsaw ghetto was in business. (April 20 was Hitler's birthday. One wonders whether the Warsaw ghetto was a birthday present to him from the German people.) We found a place to stay for the night in a barn on a farm in the outskirts of Białystok. The attic of the barn was full of dried hay—very comfortable for sleeping. The next morning, we discovered that our guide was nowhere to be found—no big loss at that point.

My mother had a heart-to-heart talk with Irenka, and strongly suggested that she return to her family's farm where she would be safer and would have food—neither of which we could guarantee. Irenka agreed with her. My mother gave her a generous "severance payment," and Irenka was off, leaving us all in tears. We never heard from Irenka again. Now we were three: me, my mother, and Dorka.

My mother decided to go and check out the town. She left Dorka and me at the farm, and off she went. She came back an hour or two later with my father in tow. Apparently, she had found a huge billboard at the town's marketplace on which anyone could post a search notice (e.g., "I am looking for Jan Mazurski from Lwów") or look to see whether a friend or family member had already posted a notice. That's what my mother did, and she found a notice from my father. She went to the address on that notice, and there he was, in his civvies, shaving. He had had enough good sense to get rid of all the medals he had won in the Polish-Soviet War of 1919-1920, along with his uniform and all the other incriminating items. When my parents came, half running, to find me and Dorka at the farm, my father's right cheek was still covered with shaving cream.

I went to a Russian kindergarten where I learned how to read and write Russian. Life calmed down for a while.

During the next year, our farmer-landlord decided that I must learn to ride a horse. That project ended when I fell off the horse onto cobblestones, and the horse kicked me in the head, leaving a half-grapefruit-size bump above my right eye. Then a kid who was somewhat older than I and did not like me (or maybe did not like people who spoke Polish, or were Jews, or both) threw half a brick at me, which hit me on the left side of my head, leaving me with two matching "half-grapefruits." Later, I was bit by a gander—that *really* hurt.

-3-
THE RUSSIAN COMMISSAR

In 1940, my parents, my aunt Dorka, and I were living in Słonim (which is now in Belarus). Our apartment had three small rooms, a kitchen, and a tiny bathroom. We lived there more or less contentedly until Germany attacked Russia in June of 1941. The only thorn in our collective hide came about as follows.

A week or two after we settled in Słonim, a Russian functionary showed up at our door, and informed us that our lodgings were too large for the four of us, so we would have to take in a lodger—in this case, the Russian government's functionary responsible for governing the Słonim region—the local Commissar.

After a few days, he showed up at the door (to my regret, I can't remember his name). He was short, somewhat shy, with a rather quiet sense of humor and, to our surprise, had relatively good manners. He came from a small town in Siberia. Since both my parents were born before World War I in the town of Kielce (which prior to World War I was in Russia), they both had gone to Russian schools and spoke fluent Russian. This was a huge help in communicating with our lodger, who was mono-lingual and barely literate. Despite some loss of individual privacy, we managed to get on together relatively well. I suspect that, because of my young age, I was less affected by all this than the adults in our group.

After a few weeks, our lodger asked my father, in my presence, to help him send a telegram. That's when we found out that our lodger had a family: a wife and two children. The telegram he dictated was to his wife, and was very brief: "Come here right away. Bring the children. Słonim is America." But even I already knew that, during World War II, *no* part of Poland was America.

The "house" we had rented for four people was now occupied by eight. Then Germany attacked Russia in 1941 (another Blitzkrieg). They occupied the entire part of Poland that the Russians had been occupying prior to that date, as well as parts of western Russia, nearly all of the Ukraine and Belarus. The Russians retreated and ran for cover, abandoning some of their troops, guns, supplies, and civilians, including our lodger and his family.

A few days after the Germans occupied Słonim, at 6 AM one morning, there was a knock at our front door. Two German officers with the dreaded SS insignia on their collars ("SS" for "Schutzstaffel," meaning Defense Corps) stood before us. The SS actually were the Nazi political state police, which operated concentration and extermination camps, and other such enterprises. They asked to see our lodger, so we asked him to come down from his room, which he did, in a nearly complete state of undress. The Germans told him to put on some pants.

He complied. The Germans took him out to the town market and shot him, for no reason that we knew. I don't know anything about what happened to our lodger's family.

-4-
AUNT DORKA

At the end of June 1941, a week before my seventh birthday, Germany attacked Russia. I watched with fear as the German soldiers ran through the fields around Słonim and shot people at random. To no one's surprise, after a few months they built a ghetto in Słonim, and then they started to carry out "sweeps," also known as "actions," picking up people in the street at random. They would triage the people: the young and the healthy were sent to labor camps; the old, the children, the infirm, the sick, the cripples, the Jews, the Gypsies, the homosexuals, and other "undesirables" to extermination camps, such as Majdanek, Trȩblinka, and Oswięcim-Birkenau (Auschwitz).

My father believed that there was safety in numbers, and that, if we were to get into a bigger ghetto, we'd be safer: "They can't kill all the Jews in the Białystok ghetto; there are too many of us there," he would say. He was wrong, but we went to Białystok anyway and smuggled ourselves *into* the ghetto there. But history repeated itself: more random sweeps, triages, and open railroad gondolas that normally carried coal, but this time hauled a human cargo to a variety of labor and extermination camps.

We made a secret hiding place in our Białystok house. It consisted of a tunnel under the house that was about 25 feet long by 3 feet wide and 4 feet high. At one end, it had a narrow ventilation slit; and at the other end, a camouflaged entry and exit trap-door located in the floor of a walk-in closet in the bedroom.

We hid there whenever we knew or suspected that a "sweep" was coming, and stayed very quiet, because the Germans and their informers developed a technique for finding hidden Jews: they would come into a house where they suspected some Jews were hiding and lie quietly on the beds, waiting for their victims to make a noise or to emerge.

My Aunt Dorka was caught in one of those

sweeps. A couple of months after World War II ended in Europe (May 7, 1945), my father went to eastern Poland to try to find out what happened to Dorka and to their brother, Heniek.

He did find two people who were in the same extermination camp as Dorka and remembered her. Both of them, independently, told my father essentially the same story: on the way to the extermination camp, Dorka met and became friendly with a woman who was pregnant and whose husband had been recently murdered. After a few days, Dorka's friend was picked to be part of the next gas-chamber-bound group. Then and there, Dorka decided to take the place of her new friend and go to the gas chamber in her friend's stead.

-5-
UNCLE HENIEK

Before World War II, my father's younger brother, Heniek (diminutive of Henry or Henryk), also lived in Warsaw. He was not married, had no family of his own, and lived alone. I got the feeling (I am not sure how) that my parents didn't entirely approve of him. I also got the impression that he was something of a playboy; he had some female friends and a dog—a Doberman Pinscher—that scared me to death.

He also had a sailboat (a sloop) that he sailed up and down the Vistula River. The Vistula is a rather wide river that originates in the south of Poland, in the Carpathian mountains, on the border between Poland and Czechoslovakia, and then flows north to the Baltic Sea, bisecting Warsaw, with the part of Warsaw called Praga (not to be confused with the Prague that is the capital of the Czech Republic) on the east, and the "real" Warsaw on the west. He also owned a private car—a rarity in Poland in those days!

I don't know what he did for a living; he may have been some sort of engineer. He was obviously doing okay for himself.

He was musically gifted; he was a very fine pianist—entirely self-taught, according to my father. I recall him playing the piano very well when he came to visit. He also played the church-style organ—pipes, keyboards, and all—quite well.

Once the Germans occupied Warsaw in 1939, he did the same thing that we did: he smuggled himself into the Russian-occupied part of Poland and ended up in a small town that happened to have a nunnery. For some reason, the nunnery had no organist. Heniek applied for the job and got it. A year and a half later, on June 22, 1941, Germany attacked Russia.

After the end of World War II in Europe, my father went to eastern Poland looking for my aunt Dorka and for Heniek. He learned that, soon after the Germans occupied that region in 1941, a German officer showed up at the nunnery and asked to see the Mother Superior.

He informed her that her organist was Jewish, which was not permitted under the laws of the Third Reich. The Mother Superior told him that, without an organist, it was very difficult to have a proper mass, and asked him to make an exception.

He thought about it and said he would let things stay as they were for now. He told her that he would let her know in a while what his final decision in this matter was, and he left.

A couple of weeks later, he reappeared with another man in tow and informed the Mother Superior that this man would henceforth be her new organist. He told her that this fellow was not only a very good organist, but he was also Aryan. He then left, taking my uncle along. No one ever heard from my uncle again.

Hearing this, my father decided to go back to Warsaw. He got on a train, sat down in an empty compartment, and was reading the paper when two men entered the compartment he was in. One of them pulled out a handgun and announced that this was a hold-up. They asked my father to hand over all his money, wedding ring, watch, wallet, and all other valuable items.

While my father was collecting all these items, he thought that, after he handed over his valuables, the robbers were sure to kill him. In those days, this was the standard *modus operandi:* no criminal wanted to leave behind any live witnesses to his or her crimes. So my father figured that he had nothing to lose. He maneuvered himself so the unarmed robber was standing between him and the gunman, and, using the unarmed robber as a shield and a ram, proceeded to shove the startled gunman out the door of the compartment onto the tracks, and then did the same thing with the other robber. During all of this, the gunman got off some shots, two of which hit my father; one bullet went through the knuckle of his right-hand middle finger, and the second went in just below his left collarbone, exiting through his left armpit and passing just an inch or so from his heart. Eventually, my father was taken to a small, primitive hospital, where his wounds were repaired and he was kept for two or three days.

He wrote a letter to my mother. Fortunately, he was ambidextrous, so he could write with either hand. The fact that his right hand was disabled did not stop him from writing, although his right and left handwritings were very different. He told a bunch of white lies: "Someone slammed a door on my right hand, so I have to write with my left hand," and so on. He came home and healed fairly quickly, although for the rest of his life his right middle finger was about half an inch shorter than both his right index and ring fingers, and it didn't bend easily.

-6-
A FORK IN THE TRACKS

Let's go back in time to Białystok. After a year or so, history repeated itself: more sweeps in the ghetto, more railroad coal gondolas with their soon-to-be-gassed human cargo, and my father still believing that safety lay in numbers. This time, we decided to go for broke: back to Warsaw and its ghetto.

We sneaked onto a Warsaw-bound freight train, and the next day we were in the Warsaw railroad yards. We watched from a distance as the Warsaw Ghetto, engulfed in flames, was having its own "final solution." The Warsaw Ghetto uprising was in full swing and lasted from April 19 to May 16, 1943.

A rapidly-developed alternate plan involved finding a friend of my father, a doctor, and asking for shelter. We eventually found him. He agreed to let us stay in his office, provided we were gone by 6 a.m., before the cleaning crew arrived, and that we didn't return until after 8 p.m., when it was dark. We needed to take a streetcar to get there. My parents boarded the streetcar through the rear platform, and I, through the front one. As the streetcar lurched into motion, I saw my mother waving to me. Her waving, I assumed, meant that we were getting off at the next stop, so at the next stop I exited the streetcar. But she had only meant to remind me that the front of the streetcar was reserved for Germans. The streetcar left with my parents still on board. This put me in a quandary; I was getting scared, but I figured that if I just followed the tracks, I would eventually find that streetcar. But then I came upon a fork in the tracks. That created another nasty conundrum. I rested my knapsack against the wall of a building, sat on it, and pondered my dilemma.

On the other side of the street was an old palace that I vaguely recognized. It might have been the royal Belweder Palace, but I am not sure. At that time, it was obviously used as some sort of headquarters for the German SS.

It had a big front gate, with a guard booth at each side of that gate, and an SS soldier in each booth. Every minute or so, the two guards exchanged places, goose-stepping in unison, their spit-polished boots glinting in the sun. They saluted each other, and then stood at attention for the next minute. I was mesmerized by this spectacle.

Eventually, reality reasserted itself and I stopped day-dreaming. I started thinking again about my situation. I decided to stay put, hoping that my parents would eventually come back. I was sure that, fate being fickle, if I continued walking along the left branch of the tracks' fork, the streetcar would have gone down the right branch, and vice versa. So I waited.

I was right. After a few minutes, I saw my parents coming. I waved to them, and they started running towards me, my mother sobbing loudly all the way. I tried to calm her down, telling her over and over again that she shouldn't attract attention to us, that it was dangerous. But to no avail.

We moved away from the palace and the German guards, and melted into the passing crowd. Another narrow escape. Without any further adventures and with great relief, we reached the doctor's office. It was a Sunday, so no cleaning crew was present. We ravenously attacked the sandwiches the doctor had kindly brought for us.

-7-
IN HIDING

We camped as best we could at our doctor friend's office for a few days, during which time my father, with help from other friends, found us a more permanent hiding place. It was in a large apple orchard in a suburb of Warsaw. Our so-called lodgings consisted of a poorly-heated shed, with no running water or toilet. We had to use an outhouse, but it was dangerous to do so during daylight hours. If you looked Jewish and were spotted by the hoodlums who were trolling for hidden Jews whom they could denounce to the Germans (and earn a per-head reward for doing so), then that would be the end for us and for those who gave us shelter. We had a very primitive camping stove for cooking. I slept on a reclining beach chair. I don't remember exactly what my parents slept on—some sort of very old couch. We had a lot of apples to eat for free. I got very good at predicting, without cutting any of the apples open, which apples' cores were beginning to rot, thereby amazing our landlords. I don't know where I learned how to do that.

My father continued to teach me, as he had done in the Słonim and Białystok ghettos. By that time, I was nearly ten years old; I had "class" every morning. My mother dyed her hair blond and, with her hazel eyes, was able to pass for an Aryan. She was our "outside person"; she did all of our shopping and other errands.

We stayed in that orchard for a year or so. During that time, my parents reconnected with some of their trusted friends and acquaintances. One such acquaintance made an offer to my father: he wanted to buy one of my paternal grandfather's apartment buildings "if the price was right." By that time, my grandfather was already dead. He had been quite well-to-do before the war, and owned several apartment buildings in Poland and other countries. My father and his acquaintance agreed on one

American Golden Eagle—a gold 20-dollar coin—as the price for that building. It wasn't much; today, the price of such a coin is about $1,200. With that money, my father bought on the black market three birth certificates that had been originally issued to a family, already deceased, that roughly matched the description of my mother, my father, and me. This became our new Aryan identity. After the war, when we were naturalized in the US, we kept the new names—there were very few people left alive who knew us by our old names. But we took our original first names as our new middle names. Thus, my original name was changed from Adam Elencwajg to Theodore Adam Dolotta.

-8-
GOODBYE, WARSAW

In mid-1944, the Russian army began approaching Warsaw from the east, and was set to attack "Fortress Warsaw," but the Germans decided to resist them at all cost. As a response to this, the Polish underground army started an uprising on August 1 to help expel the Germans from Warsaw and from Poland. But once the Polish underground forces started the uprising, the Russians stopped their attacks on the German forces, and just watched the Germans and Poles kill each other off.

This uprising lasted sixty-three days, and then the Polish underground forces capitulated.

Shortly before this uprising, we had reconnected with a woman by the name of Marysia Dobrostańska. Before the war, she used to be a seamstress, and she made all of my mother's clothes. We trusted her unconditionally. Later, she saved our lives by arranging for us to hide with her Aryan, anti-Semitic family in the town of Chęstochowa. We stayed with her until the war was almost over.

During the uprising, there were many dead human bodies, and a few dead horses, all around. The dead horses became food, while burial details were needed to bury the dead. My father was recruited into such a burial detail. As for me, I got sick with some terrible disease that lasted for a few weeks. There were no doctors to diagnose it, but rumor had it that it was typhus. We had to move daily, as buildings were shelled and bombed all around us.

After the Warsaw uprising, the Germans proceeded to evacuate the entire population of Warsaw to a nearby small concentration camp, which served as a triage center. We were forced to get there on foot.

The Germans then proceeded to systematically burn down whole sections of the city, one after the other, with flame throwers. (After the war, almost all of Warsaw had to be re-surveyed before it could be rebuilt: it was simply impossible to tell, without re-surveying the entire city, where most of the streets had been before the war. I have heard that this work is now done, and that Warsaw has been rebuilt almost exactly as it was before World War II.)

Once in the triage camp, we were housed in large barracks, and the triage started: able-bodied adults to one side, all other people to the other side. The two groups were then loaded onto separate railroad trains: the first group to labor camps, the other to extermination camps. My mother managed to convince a German officer to allow all three of us to go with the able-bodied group.

The German war machine was beginning to sputter and show signs of wear and tear. Our train was slow, it stopped often, traveled in circles, and people were able to jump off and run away.

There were groups of peasants, standing along the tracks, tossing food into the passing railroad gondolas. Fights erupted over who would get this loaf of bread, or that piece of sausage. I managed to grab a big yellow onion which I ate ravenously, skin and all. I threw it up a while later.

I remember being very cold. Despite the

fact it was only October, it was below freezing—a Polish winter. I eventually fell asleep on the floor of the railroad car.

When I woke up a few hours later, my right leg hurt and was itching. I realized I had wet myself, and that the urine had frozen to my skin. I had no socks, and I got a case of frostbite. (From then on, whenever it got cold, the itching returned. It took about twenty years for the frostbite itch to disappear completely.)

The next evening, the train made a stop at a railroad station to take on some water for the steam locomotive. At first, in the dark, my parents did not recognize the station, but eventually they did. We were in Kielce, the town where both of my parents were raised; we had to get out of there before anyone recognized them. Our horrible trip had gotten even worse.

All of us, including Marysia, got on another southbound freight train as soon as we could. That evening, we arrived in Chęstochowa, a mid-sized town southwest of Warsaw, and the holiest town in Poland. The cathedral there houses the painting of the Black Madonna that is credited with many miracles. Also,

Marysia had family there. She told us to keep secret from her family the fact we were Jewish, because she did not trust them. So I became a deaf girl—a girl to avoid the circumcision test, and deaf so it wouldn't seem odd that I stayed in our room and didn't come out to play with the other neighborhood children. (By the way, pretending to be deaf is almost impossible: try not to flinch or jump when someone unexpectedly drops something, or claps their hands, behind your back.) So on the whole, I found safety in staying in our room. Fortunately, the pitch of my voice was still high enough to not betray me as being a boy.

On occasion, so as not to raise suspicions, my parents and I went to Catholic mass on Sunday, as did most Poles in Chęstochowa. On one Sunday, we went to the cathedral where the painting of the Black Madonna was displayed. My parents told me that, whenever I crossed from one side of the cathedral to the other, I should genuflect and cross myself when passing in front of that painting. I did this as instructed on this occasion, but with my back to the altar and to the Madonna painting. I thought that my mother was going to have a heart attack when she saw me doing this. Fortunately, no one raised an alarm.

-9-
THE YOUNG SOLDIER

It was March or early April of 1945, the last few weeks of World War II, which ended in Europe with the surrender of Germany. We were still hiding in Chęstochowa with Marysia Dobrostańska.

Many of the Wehrmacht (German army) units that had been fighting the Russians on the eastern front were retreating through the Chęstochowa area under constant Russian fire.

One day, a German army supply train arrived at the local railroad station. After its crew abandoned the train, the local populace began looting it. We joined the crowd, and I snagged a very nice leather first-aid kit.

Another day, a German Howitzer battery parked in front of our house. The German crew jumped off the Howitzer carriers, threw themselves on the ground, and started swallowing as much snow as they could. They were obviously extremely thirsty; they must have driven non-stop for a very long time. My mother looked through a window at them and said, angrily and to no one in particular, "God is punishing them. They deserve it." This was a harsh thing for her to say. I was very surprised.

The Germans set up the Howitzers to shoot at the advancing Russians, who shot back. We figured we were done for, because at least some of the Russian artillery shells were bound to miss the German Howitzers and hit our house. If we tried to run away it would likely result in a bullet in each of our heads. So we sat in the basement of the house and waited for we knew not what.

When it got dark, the Germans climbed back onto their Howitzer carriers and headed west, leaving our area of the city a no man's land. We tried to get some sleep. I think I was the only one who actually fell asleep; I was eleven years old.

The next morning, no one was to be seen in the streets—no Germans, no Poles, no Russians, no one. It was indeed a no man's land. I decided to go and check out the territory (of course, without telling my parents; they would have surely vetoed this project). It was eerily quiet.

I walked past two houses and turned onto a side street, only to be met by a horrible sight: lying in the snow on the sidewalk was a German soldier in his boots and his gray-green Wehrmacht great coat, soaked in blood, with his helmet and rifle next to him in the snow, his bright, blue eyes wide open. He could not have been older than fourteen or fifteen.

He was very dead. His body had been run over by the tread of a tank. His chest was gone, and I could see the tread-marks where his chest had been. I ran home.

To this day, I cannot forgive myself for not having had the common decency to close his eyelids.

-10-
VE DAY

On April 30, 1945, Hitler and Eva Braun (Hitler's mistress whom he married the previous day) both committed suicide, and on May 8 (Victory-in-Europe Day, or VE Day), Germany surrendered unconditionally to the Allies. At the time, we were still in Chęstochowa, now occupied by Russians. There was no radio, no newspapers, no outside communication. The Russians had attached loudspeakers to some of the telephone poles on the main street corners to broadcast whatever news there was.

I was outside when I heard that Germany had surrendered. I ran into the house and told my parents. They did not believe me at first. Then pandemonium ensued and people were singing, dancing, praying, embracing each other. We were still alive and, we believed, safe. That night, we went to sleep without fear in our hearts for the first time in years. We were so happy.

And giving credit where credit is due, I must say that I am absolutely certain that my survival was entirely due to the loving, mental, emotional, and physical support of my parents throughout the entire war. I was very lucky.

-11-
BACK TO WARSAW

Shortly after the end of the war, my parents decided to move back to Warsaw. This was rather difficult; as I mentioned earlier, Warsaw had been almost completely destroyed by the Germans after they put down the Polish underground's uprising, which lasted from August 1 to October 2, 1944. It is estimated that by January 1945, 85 percent of Warsaw was totally destroyed. When World War II ended in Europe on May 8, 1945, we were still in Chęstochowa. About a month later, we did move back to Warsaw. The trip took a few days—no trains, roads full of bomb craters, and so on.

At that point, we had some good luck. Before the war, my paternal grandfather owned several apartment buildings in Warsaw and its suburbs. All of these buildings, other than a small, single-apartment house that was his home, were completely destroyed. After the war, his home at 21 Szustra Street was not occupied, but all of his furniture was still there. We simply moved in.

I did some rummaging in that house and, in a closet, I found about three-and-a-half-million paper tsarist rubles. Before World War I, that was an immense fortune. By the time I found it, it was worthless. My grandfather was something of a serial fortune maker: the tsarist money I found was his first fortune, pre-World War I. All the real estate he acquired between World War I and World War II was his second major fortune. He died after the start of World War II.

Then some more good luck came our way, probably helped by the fact that, tragically, the Germans had killed a large percentage of lawyers in Poland. My father was appointed the head of the legal department of the Ministry of Food and Agriculture. It was a relatively prestigious position, and it helped us to eventually get out of Poland. It also helped with more mundane matters: the Ministry of Food and

Agriculture looked out after "its own." Once a week a small truck drove up to our house and dropped off food: flour, potatoes, vegetables, a bit of meat on occasion, small amounts of milk, butter, cheese, fruit, and so forth.

After the malnutrition of the previous several years, it was indeed manna from heaven.

-12-
NEW EXODUS

Our life started to drift towards normalcy, albeit quite slowly. My parents enrolled me in a public elementary school, while warning me still not to tell anyone that I was Jewish, for fear of more persecution. I also joined the Polish Boy Scouts.

But then, after a year, all hell broke loose again, this time in the town of Kielce. Both of my parents were raised in Kielce, which is located roughly halfway between Warsaw and Kraków. On the fourth of July, 1946, fourteen months after the end of World War II in Europe, the Kielce Pogrom occurred. In 1939, there were approximately 24,000 Jewish inhabitants in Kielce, or one-third of the town's population. Almost all of them were murdered during the Holocaust. By the summer of 1946, about two hundred Jews, who were Holocaust survivors, had returned and resettled in Kielce. During the pogrom 42 of them were killed and 40 were wounded.[1,2]

It was the deadliest pogrom in Poland against Jews since World War II. This pogrom was the most significant event in the history of Polish Jewry. It took place just over a year after the end of World War II and of the Holocaust, traumatizing not only the few Jews left in Poland, but most Jews left in the world. It was the catalyst for the flight from Poland of many, if not most, of the few remaining Polish Jews who had survived the Holocaust.

My parents and I were part of this modern-day Exodus. My father's position at the Ministry of Food and Agriculture gave him access to authorities who issued passports, so he got us three passports. He also got us 24-hour transit visas through Czechoslovakia, through two of the four zones of Germany that we needed to cross, and through France. (Immediately after World War II, Germany was divided into four zones, with each zone governed by one of the following: USSR, France, Great Britain, and the USA.) But no visas to the USA could be obtained that easily; that took years to acquire.

Another ace up our collective sleeve was the then current informal policy of the Polish Government—which, at that time, was a Socialist coalition government—to allow all Jews and other Holocaust survivors in Poland to emigrate, with essentially no questions asked. So we got on a train and left. We spent the first night and the first day of our trip acting like tourists in Prague, the capital of Czechoslovakia. I found a store selling Czech Boy Scout uniforms and bought myself a really nice Czech Boy Scout belt.

We spent the next two days on the train. We didn't leave the train for fear of not being allowed to get back on. Our train went through Nuremberg, where the World War II war-crime trials were going on. They were organized and run by the IMT (the International Military Tribunal). The judges and prosecutors were appointed by the four wartime Allies.

Finally, we arrived in Paris, where Cecily (one of my mother's two surviving siblings, of the original eight) lived with her family; they had left Poland before World War II. They took us in for a while, helped us convert our twenty-four-hour French transit visas into six-year residence visas, got us food coupons (being younger than sixteen, I even got milk coupons), and so on. I enrolled in high school (Lycée Jacques Decour, Paris 9ème), and joined the French Boy Scouts, known as "Eclaireurs" — literally "Road Illuminators."

I learned French, and made a small number of very good friends. I also became very fond of a soda drink called "diabolo à la menthe" (soda water with mint syrup), and of "croissants patissiers" (pastry-shop-style croissants). I also went on several occasions to the Paris Opera and the Paris Opera Comique, to the Comedie Française, and to other theaters. I saw *Cyrano de Bergerac* on one occasion.

During summers, I went to Boy Scout camps. One year, I went to a camp in the Alps on the Swiss border — great chocolate! Another summer, I went to the beaches of Normandy in the area that was the scene of D-Day, still full of WWII mementos such as machine-gun pillboxes, with those guns still loaded with nine-yard belts of live ammunition; I believe that this is where the expression "the whole nine yards" comes from, as in "I sprayed that tank with the whole nine yards.") We had a lot of fun practicing target shooting. We also gathered mussels and clams on the beach that we boiled for lunch and ate, accompanied by cider.

Occasionally, we even found a cider vendor who would sell us some "hard" cider. Add a crisp baguette or two, and we had us some great meals.

During another summer, I went to Scouting's World Jamboree. There were scouts from forty or so countries, including a big contingent from the USA—the US scouts were easy to spot, because, to the amusement of all other attendees, they wore long pants.

So all in all, my five years in France—compared with the previous seven years in Poland—were a *vast* improvement. The differences are almost impossible to describe, but it should not surprise anyone that, mostly as a result of these differences, I am something of a Francophile. It was nice not to have to be afraid all the time.

And while I was learning French—as well as a great deal about French food, from Camembert to Cassoulet to Choucroute Garnie to Crème Fraîche and Éclairs au Chocolat—my world kept moving along and improving in the process. In 1950, I received the diploma certifying that I had completed the first cycle (five years) of high school; French high school lasted seven years, divided into two cycles; the first, five years, and the second, two.

In early 1950, miracle of miracles, we received our resident (permanent) visas to the United States. This process had taken over five years from when we left Poland in 1945. We wasted no time. We received enough money to buy steamship tickets for the three of us from a charitable organization called the United Jewish Appeal (UJA) that was helping so-called "displaced persons" restart their lives after World War II.

We took the train from Paris to the French port of Le Havre, and boarded the Holland America steamship Veendam. We got a three-bed cabin—a pair of bunk beds plus a single bed. (I got the upper bunk.) The ship stopped in Southampton, England, for a few hours to take on some more passengers, and then we were off across the Atlantic to "the land of the free and the home of the brave."

For me, it was an exhilarating feeling. We

were out of Europe, the land of World War II.

The trip across the Atlantic was scheduled for seven-and-a-half days, but it took eleven-and-a-half. The weather was absolutely atrocious. The baggage master broke one of his legs. The fiddler—who, with the piano player, provided music for dinner—fell down and cracked his head; he wore a turban-like bandage for the rest of the trip. All of the deck furniture was washed overboard. We had to eat in our cabins, because most of the glass in the dining room windows and portholes was smashed. Besides all of this, most passengers were violently seasick.

A couple of days after our departure, we learned that two ships, similar to ours and following us by a day or so, each had a fatality on board from falls. At one point, our ship was pitching so violently that when I stood on the rear deck and looked above the top of the *rear* smoke stack, I could see sea water *above* that smoke stack. In a lounge, there was a map showing our progress. Our ship's path was plotted on it, with dots marking our position at noon each day. During this storm, three or four of these dots were on top of each other, because the ship was sitting in one spot, just maneuvering to avoid capsizing.

The next day, my father woke me up very early; the sun was just rising. He told me to get dressed. After I did, we went out on deck. The sea was finally calm, and our ship was gliding up the Hudson River, past the Statue of Liberty towards the Holland-America pier in Hoboken.

I thought we had *finally* arrived in the *real* America, and *not* the America that our lodger in Słonim, the Russian Commissar, imagined. The poor man never knew how wrong he was.

-13-
EPILOGUE

My parents and I had a number of good years after we moved to the USA, although my parents had to work very hard. Both of them were lawyers, but since they did not speak English, they couldn't practice law in America. So they took out a mortgage and bought an egg farm in Vineland, New Jersey. Egg farming is *horribly* hard work, especially for middle-aged, sedentary people. But the Leghorn chickens do not care what language the farmers do, or do not, speak. After several years, my parents retired.

We also kept in touch with Marysia Dobrostańska. She was still living in Poland with a couple of her nieces. My parents started sending her packages of food, but these shipments kept getting stolen in transit. So we switched from food to paper money. If the paper money was wrapped in plain, opaque paper before being put in an envelope, it got through to Marysia. We were amazed when she told us how much one hundred dollars would buy on the black market in Poland in those days.

After my mother died, I took over the operation of this monthly "money express." Eventually, Marysia died, and her niece wrote to thank me and to explain how vitally important the monthly cash gifts were to Marysia. She said they gave Marysia a sense of dignity: not only was she not a burden to her family, she was a valued financial contributor to her family's well-being.

As for me, after we came to the States, I went to high school for one year to learn some English—first to summer school at Glenville High School in Cleveland, Ohio, where I stayed with my Aunt Regina, and then, for the rest of that year, to Vineland High School in Vineland, New Jersey, while also keeping in good repair the water fountains in our chicken coops. I then went to college, majoring in Physics, and to graduate school, where I got a PhD in Computer Science. While I was still in graduate school, I met and married the love of my life, Barbara.

(I wish to say that throughout my school years, be it in France or the USA, I was most fortunate to have a number of teachers, in high schools, university, and graduate school, who took an interest in and mentored me, easing my transition from one language to another, and then a third. They helped me adjust to the new and different scholastic environments. To them all, I hereby offer my gratitude and my thanks.)

Then, I was on the faculty and staff of Princeton University for seven years, and subsequently worked for several companies. First, I founded a small software start-up called Princeton Time Sharing Services. I then worked for Bell Telephone Laboratories, and then for Interactive Systems Corporation, another small software start-up in Los Angeles. Finally, I worked for SoftBank, a Japanese company. I eventually retired in 2004. I have three sons and five grandchildren. My dear wife, Barbara, to whom I was married for fifty-four years, passed away in 2014.

Looking back in time, in 1962 I went back to France — this time with my wife — on a postdoctoral fellowship sponsored by NATO. We did a bit of traveling, and on one train trip, we were in a compartment with two other couples, one English and the other French, as well as a young man about eighteen to twenty years old, and we were chatting among the three couples.

The young man was not saying a word. Trying to make him feel more comfortable, I asked him where he was from. He looked down at his shoes, paused for a moment, and then said, very softly, "I'm sorry. I am German." I felt very sad for him.

My mother died in 1981 from Alzheimer's disease. By then, we were living in Princeton, New Jersey. A few months after her death, my family and I moved to Los Angeles.

In 1983, my father, who was then eighty-three, followed us to California, driving alone from New Jersey to Los Angeles in seven days, his bicycle securely strapped to the roof of his station wagon, "just in case." He first learned to drive at the age of fifty-one. I got my driving license that same year, at the age of seventeen.

In 1995, I had to put my father in a home for Alzheimer's sufferers. That home was a very nice and very well-run place. But over the next six or seven months, my father managed to escape from that home nine or ten times, the first time by climbing onto, and then jumping off the other side of an eight-foot-tall cement-block wall. During one such escapade, I got a phone call at my office from a very nice-sounding lady who said she was at a five and ten cent store where my father approached her. She told me he was dressed very nicely and asked her for help. He told her that he had just escaped from a concentration camp and needed to get to Berlin, and could she help him buy a railroad ticket to get there. He gave her his name, as well as my name and phone number (he was not all that demented). He also became well-known to almost the entire Santa Monica police force, which spent a lot of time looking for him. He began stealing and hiding knives from the nursing home's dining room, and collecting bricks and stones with which he tried to attack members of the nursing home's staff.

I made a deal with the cashier of a nice Jewish deli on Wilshire Boulevard in Santa Monica, which my father liked a lot—Fromin's, at 19th Street, next door to the five and ten cent store I mentioned above. The deal was that, any time the cashier saw my father, she would call me and I would come and take him home.

Although some days he did not recognize me at all, on one visit, he told me that he hated being back in the extermination camp (!) where all the "guards" (the staff of the nursing home) were "going to kill me." That explained the reason for all his escape attempts. To me, it was heart-breaking.

My father died at ninety-five years of age on October 6, 1995, at Saint John's Hospital in Santa Monica, California, of old age. His life had been a long trip indeed, from Kielce in Poland to Kiev in the Ukraine to Santa Monica, California. I watched as his ashes were scattered into the Pacific Ocean.

-14-
PHOTOS

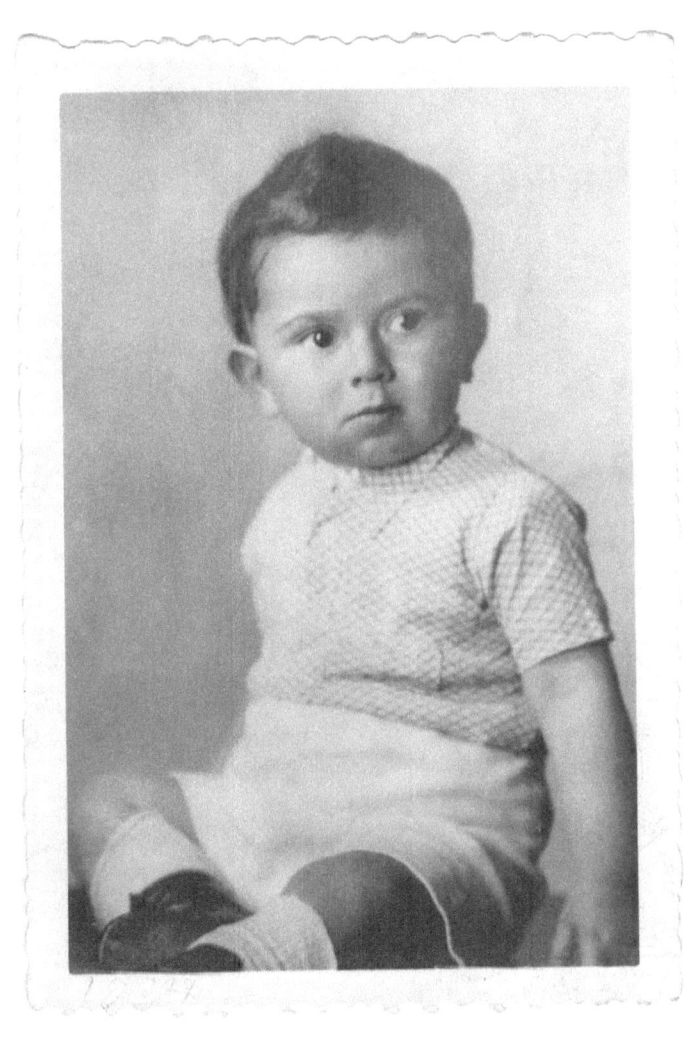

Author, Adam Elencwajg,
at age 2, 1936

Author's Aunt, Dwojra (Dorka) Elencwajg, in Białystok, 1940

Author's Family (Left to Right): Mother Dwojra Elencwajg, Grandmother Hannah Elencwajg, Nanny Irenka, Father Nathan Elencwajg, and Aunt Dwojra Elencwajg, 1932

Author with his parents
on arrival in Paris, 1946

Author in Paris, 1949

Author with his Mother (Left) and his Aunt Regina, on arrival in New York, 1951.

-15-
MAP OF THE RELEVANT AREA

-16- REFERENCES

1. Google: "Kielce Pogrom." The first two articles that appear—"The Kielce Pogrom: A Blood Libel Massacre of Holocaust Survivors" and "Kielce pogrom—Wikipedia"—provide a comprehensive overview of the Kielce Pogrom.

2. *Fear: Anti-Semitism in Poland after Auschwitz* by Jan T. Gross. Copyright © 2006 by Jan T. Gross. Published by Random House, New York.

3. *Neighbors: The Destruction of the Jewish Community in Jedwabne, Poland* by Jan T. Gross. Copyright © 2001 by Princeton University Press, New Jersey.

4. *Wartime Lies: a Novel* by Louis Begley. Copyright © 1991 by Louis Begley. Published by Ballantine Books, New York.

5. "The Last Trial — A great-grandmother, Auschwitz, and the arc of justice" by Elizabeth Kolbert. Letter from Berlin, *The New Yorker*, February 16, 2015.

6. "Portrait of a Wily Holocaust Survivor," *The New York Times,* January 24, 2014, pp. 16-17.

7. *Anne Frank – the Diary of a Young Girl* by Anne Frank. Copyright © 1952 by Anne Frank. Published by Bantam Books, New York.

www.ingramcontent.com/pod-product-compliance
Lightning Source LLC
Chambersburg PA
CBHW021132300426
44113CB00006B/394